KINGS

Don't Settle

A BOOK OF POEMS TO EMPOWER MEN

DESH DIXON

ISBN 10: 9781090555601

DEDICATION

This book is for all of my Kings around the world. You are Kings gentlemen. It is my hope and intention that you are encouraged, inspired and empowered to acknowledge the King in you. Own your Kingness, your highness.

CONTENTS

CONTENTS

ACKNOWLEDGMENTS

I would like to thank all of my fans and supporters around the world. I would like to thank my true friends and family for their support. I want to acknowledge my Kings out there who are doing the work and stepping up to embody Kingness. Thank you for showing the world that good men still exist.

YOUR CHOICE: KEEP SETTLING
OR KING UP

Gentlemen, it's time to take your rightful place back upon your throne. No matter what you've been through or any past mistakes, you are still a beautiful child of God. You are a King. You have always been regal. Kings are royalty. It's time to hold your head high and step back into your power. You are worthy and deserving of all your hearts desires.

1 KINGNESS TIP

Don't shrink for anyone! You are a King. No one can denounce your title but you. Shine bright in all your magnificence.

<u>Be Unapologetic</u>

King, be unapologetic

You're immaculate, Kingness at its best

Be proud of all that you have accomplished

Don't let the Kingless come at you with their mess.

Don't downplay any of your gifts and talents

These are God's blessings, give them the life they need

There is someone who needs you to keep going

To inspire them whoever that may be.

Don't shrink, you're way too wide-ranging

Don't minimize who you are to fit in

There will always be people who don't like you

Brush them off, keep your character from within.

Keep your values, a King must have discipline

His character will be tested many times

His maturity will remain through each hurdle

He overcomes everything easily without a fight.

King, you do not have to apologize

For your grind, your faith or your success

Reign in your Kingness unapologetically

Stay true to yourself, people can't compete with the best.

1 KINGNESS REFLECTION

Think about a time when you felt you couldn't be yourself and had to minimize who you are. How did that make you feel? Do you believe shrinking is helping you maximize your life or minimize it? Marianne Williamson mentions that there's nothing enlightened about shrinking so that other people won't feel insecure around you. Be Unapologetic! What are some things you can do to live bigger as your authentic self?

_____

_____

_____

_____

_____

_____

_____

_____

2 KINGNESS TIP

King, don't let society make you think you're less than just because you're not keeping up with the Joneses.

A King's Confidence

King, when you look into the mirror

Are you happy with exactly what you see?

It's easy to feel like you are lacking

When your life isn't where you want it to be.

Don't fret, you are still a man of honor

Your character isn't flawed or at stake

There may be things that you need to acknowledge

Rest assured, everyone's made some mistakes.

Build your confidence by honoring your calling

Follow through on the commitments that you make

Show up for yourself and your loved ones

You are responsible for the life you create.

Be a man of your word and do not waver

Your confidence is tied to your self-love

When you know who you are and don't deny it

There is nothing that you can't rise above.

King, don't forget you are royalty

You're powerful way more than you think

Your confidence should be at its highest

Your belief is the only missing link.

2 KINGNESS REFLECTION

Your worth as a man isn't tied to how much money you currently make. There's a quote that says 'no one can make you feel inferior without your consent.' You have to love yourself regardless of what's in your bank account right now or your current circumstances. Love what you see in the mirror. You may not be where you want to be but the important thing is that you're progressing. Write down some positive affirmations to say to yourself out loud when you look in the mirror. Ex: I love myself, I am wealthy, I'm successful, etc.

_____

_____

_____

_____

_____

_____

_____

_____

3 KINGNESS TIP

Stay true to yourself. Don't try to fit in. Stop seeking approval from others and be your authentic self.

Your Kingness

Kings, your work here is important

God placed you on earth for a reason

Every person that comes into your life

May only be around for a season.

Don't feel bad for making some changes

Don't put your Kinghood at stake

Let go of anyone that threatens it

Losing your kingdom will be a huge mistake.

You deserve all of God's riches and abundance

You deserve to live life as you will

You deserve to be loved and respected

Just remember you have a purpose to fulfill.

We need all of your gifts and talents

We need you to show up as a King

When you own who you are and what God gave you

There's no limit to the wealth it will bring.

King, be the man that God created

You are strong, you can handle anything that comes

You are protected and God chose you to lead

Honor your Kingness as it's a gift from heaven above.

3 KINGNESS REFLECTION

Be yourself. Be your authentic self. Stop trying to please others. There's a saying that one sure way to failure is trying to please everyone. It's impossible. The right people will love you as you are. They need you as you are, not an imitation. How do you show up in the world as your authentic self? If you don't, what needs to change in your life for you to do so?

_____
_____
_____
_____
_____
_____
_____
_____

4 KINGNESS TIP

Prepare for what you're asking for.

Your Queen

Kings, your Queen is no peasant

She's a woman of high class with great charm

She marvels in all of her grandeur

It's a blessing for you to have her on your arm.

Her love is a gift for you to cherish

Her heart is something dear for you to hold

Her soul is an essence for you to care for

Between her legs is what gives life worth more than gold.

Your Queen expects the best with no apologies

She's waiting for you to show up as the King

She needs you to embrace all of your duties

She'll say yes when you present her with the ring.

Your Queen wants to love you with no hesitation

But she must know you will fight for her love

A good woman is a prize to a good man

She is truly a gift from above.

What she wants is your love and your loyalty

She should never have to question what you do

She will always be there as your Queen

She'll stand behind you no matter what you're going through.

Kings, be the person you'd want to marry

Your Queen, she awaits on her throne

Prepare yourself and your kingdom

And soon you'll have a Queen to take home.

4 KINGNESS REFLECTION

King, what you are seeking is seeking you. If you want a Queen, are you doing things in alignment with her arrival in your life? What are some things that you're doing to be ready for her?

_____

_____

_____

_____

_____

_____

_____

_____

5 KINGNESS TIP

You are strong.

Knight (Didactic Cinquain poem)

Knight

Protective, strong

Fighting, securing, shielding

Takes care of home

Gallant.

5 KINGNESS REFLECTION

You were built to protect. How do you think a man should protect those he loves?

_____

_____

_____

_____

_____

_____

_____

_____

6 KINGNESS TIP

You can be a great lover if you choose to be.

Lover (Didactic Cinquain poem)

Lover

Romantic, chivalrous

Loving, kissing, caressing

Aims to please her

Suitor.

6 KINGNESS REFLECTION

You have the ability to be who you want. If you want to be a great lover, ask your partner about how you can be great for her. When is the last time you communicated with your partner about her needs?

_____
_____
_____
_____
_____
_____
_____
_____

7 KINGNESS TIP

Don't be afraid of your power. Own it. King up!

<u>Your Role</u>

They say a man's job is to protect and provide

So if you're asked a question, you should have nothing to hide.

A man must remember he is head of the house

He must lead by example and take care of his spouse.

You must lead from the front, set the tone from the start

Your leadership determines if it works or falls apart.

You don't have to be perfect, just accountable to your role

A happy life and a happy family should be your ultimate goal.

You're a man, you're the King

You're the one that leads the way

So if you do not have a vision

Don't be surprised that people don't stay.

Your role as King is a gift from God

Don't take it lightly, many envy your job.

7 KINGNESS REFLECTION

King up! Own that King in you. You set the standard. How are you going to show up in the world from now on and own your role?

_____

_____

_____

_____

_____

_____

_____

_____

8 KINGNESS TIP

You're perfect for the right woman.

She's Waiting

She's waiting for you

To do what you do

All day long

She's been playing your song.

Thinking about you and your sexy talk

Turned on by your swag and the way that you walk.

She never knew she could feel this way

Just continued to pray

Knowing you'd show up some day.

She knew God had the perfect King

Who'd make her say yes when presented with a ring.

She smiles with every thought of you

She blushes from this love being so true.

She can't wait to be in your arms again

You're not only her lover but her best friend

And the love between the two of you will never end.

She's waiting for you in that little black dress

Getting anxious from knowing where your hands will caress.

She's the woman for you without a doubt

So bring your A game and go all out.

A queen like her is in demand

It'd be easy for her to get a new man.

So please understand she chose you to love

Be grateful for such a gift from above.

She's waiting for you

Now what are you going to do?

Remember you're the King

So you better come through.

8 KINGNESS REFLECTION

What would it feel like to know that special someone is waiting for you? Begin to imagine this and feel the feelings as if it already existed. Your feelings will help draw in the things you want in your life. Do you believe that she is out there?

_____

_____

_____

_____

_____

_____

_____

_____

9 KINGNESS TIP

Think highly of yourself. You're a King. If you think lowly of yourself, people will treat you that way. Increase your self-love and maintain a positive perception of yourself. You are worthy.

King (Parts of Speech poem)

A King,

  Royal and Exquisite,

    Protects and Serves,

      Supremely,

        Patriarch.

9 KINGNESS REFLECTION

You are a King. What you think of yourself is important. How do you honestly perceive yourself?

_____

_____

_____

_____

_____

_____

_____

_____

10 KINGNESS TIP

You shouldn't have to give up your goals and dreams to be with someone.
You deserve to be with someone who supports them.

<u>Working Kings (5 W's poem)</u>

Kings

Work towards their goals

Everyday

Around the world

To support their loved ones.

10 KINGNESS REFLECTION

The right person will complement you. They will support you. They will be an addition, not a subtraction. What is something you refuse to settle for with your next partner?

_____

_____

_____

_____

_____

_____

_____

_____

11 KINGNESS TIP

Don't forget who you are.

A King (Cinquain poem)

A King

Is majestic

He puts his queen's needs first

God is at the center of all

Hero.

11 KINGNESS REFLECTION

Always believe in yourself. What is something you can do to remind yourself of how great you are?

_____

_____

_____

_____

_____

_____

_____

12 KINGNESS TIP

Great men exist. You're one of them.

<u>Men (Parts of Speech poem)</u>

Men,

Prominent and Powerful,

Reigns and Domineers,

Assertively,

Kings.

12 KINGNESS REFLECTION

Queens desire Kings. A Queen wants a King that is confident in who he is. What are some qualities you desire in your Queen?

_____

_____

_____

_____

_____

_____

_____

_____

13 KINGNESS TIP

A man is important to the world.

Man (Parts of Speech poem)

A Man,

Masculine and Noble,

Champions and Supports,

Wonderfully,

Himself.

13 KINGDOM REFLECTION

A man that is masculine is attractive to many women. Do you consider yourself an alpha or beta male and why?

_____
_____
_____
_____
_____
_____
_____
_____

14 KINGNESS TIP

If you want better friends, get rid of the toxic ones. If you want better furniture, get rid of the old furniture. Make space for what you're asking for. New things can't come to you if there's no room for them.

Dream Home (Cinquain poem)

Dream Home

Envision it

Grind until you get it

You deserve this dream home of yours

For you.

14 KINGNESS REFLECTION

Have you done your spring cleaning? It may not be spring but the concept remains the same. You can't expect new and better things when you keep clinging onto the old stuff. Also, you shouldn't expect more when you're ungrateful and don't take care of what you currently have. How do you take care of your current home or living space?

_____

_____

_____

_____

_____

_____

_____

_____

15 KINGNESS TIP

Do not minimize who you are to appease anyone. Your vision is your vision. God gave it to you. Your dreams are your dreams. Stop letting other people dictate how you choose to live your life. You're a King. Enough said.

<u>Your Life (Cinquain poem)</u>

Your life

Is a blessing

You matter, it matters

Know you're loved and we need you here

Sacred.

15 KINGNESS REFLECTION

It's never too late to pursue your goals and dreams. What is something you've always dreamt of doing?

_____

_____

_____

_____

_____

_____

_____

_____

16 KINGNESS TIP

Your son will follow your example. Be sure it's a good one.

<u>Son (Parts of Speech poem)</u>

Son,

  Major and sovereign,

    Safeguards and rules,

      Lordly,

        Heir.

16 KINGDOM REFLECTION

Do as I say and not as I do does not work. Your son will model what he sees. Are you leading by example?

_____

_____

_____

_____

_____

_____

_____

_____

17 KINGNESS TIP

You're the first man that your daughter interacts with. Be sure you are the example of a good one.

Daughter (Parts of Speech poem)

Daughter,

Feminine and superior,

Heightens and elevates,

Rightfully,

Queen.

17 KINGNESS REFLECTION

The relationship you have with your daughter sets the tone for the men she chooses when she gets older. What are your actions teaching your daughter about men?

_____

_____

_____

_____

_____

_____

_____

_____

18 KINGNESS TIP

Be a man of honor.

Gentleman (Parts of Speech poem)

A Gentleman,

Respectful and Considerate,

Loves and Honors,

Admirably,

Nobleman.

18 KINGNESS REFLECTION

Men should love themselves and uphold their values. Is it important to you to be a gentleman? Why or why not?

_____

_____

_____

_____

_____

_____

_____

_____

19 KINGNESS TIP

You are far too special and unique to try to be someone you're not. Never dishonor yourself.

<u>Be Yourself</u>

I know sometimes you feel

Like your kindness makes you weak

You constantly get overlooked

From some women and other things you seek.

You question what it is

And why this keeps happening to you

It makes you feel unloved

You don't know what else that you can do.

King, just be yourself

You are perfect as you are

You're a perfect child of God

With all your flaws, imperfections and scars.

You don't have to follow the crowd

You are unique and can stand alone

You don't need a bunch of fake people

Disrupting your energy so protect your throne.

The right people will always love you

They want and need you as you are

So don't change to try to impress others

Being yourself is what sets you apart.

The way you walk, the way you talk

Your values and different style

A man like you with such a giving heart

That's willing to go the extra mile.

It may seem like your kind is rare

It may look like no one seems to care.

I assure you people appreciate your type

Stay true to yourself, don't believe the hype.

Honor who you are in everything that you do

Remain strong, courageous and bold

Be yourself even when the world tries to say no

Embrace who you are, bare naked soul.

19 KINGNESS REFLECTION

Trying to be someone you're not is inauthentic not to mention exhausting. What advice would you give to your younger self?

_____

_____

_____

_____

_____

_____

_____

_____

20 KINGNESS TIP

You're royalty. Act like it.

<u>Monarch (Parts of Speech poem)</u>

The Monarchy,

Dignified and Imperial,

Shines and Emanates,

Royally,

Itself.

20 KINGNESS REFLECTION

Embrace the King that you are. What does it mean to you to be royalty?

_____

_____

_____

_____

_____

_____

_____

_____

21 KINGNESS TIP

You deserve whatever your heart desires. Don't let the world tell you otherwise.

Dream Car

The perfect toy with an engine to roar

You can't wait to put that pedal to the floor.

You dream of it more than you want to admit

So to attract this car, you have to make a mental shift.

Your dream car it is, what a sight to see

And yours it will be once you change your beliefs.

You deserve your dream car but you've got to let go

Of negative beliefs and the lies you've been told.

There is nothing special that you have to do

Just visualize and believe it was made for you.

Having your dream car, consider it done

Expect it to show up and it will come.

And once it comes, hit the road and have some fun!

21 KINGNESS REFLECTION

You can have what you want. Don't let anyone make you feel bad for wanting more than what is considered normal or status quo. What is something you've always wanted?

_____
_____
_____
_____
_____
_____
_____
_____

22 KINGNESS TIP

You're enough, King. You never know who you're inspiring. Keep moving forward.

King (5 W's poem)

A glorious King

Summoning from his throne

At the start of each day

In his palace

To keep order in the kingdom.

22 KINGNESS REFLECTION

There's a quote that says "You inspire people who pretend not to even see you." Name 1 person that you've inspired in some way no matter who they are or how old they are. How did that make you feel?

_____

_____

_____

_____

_____

_____

_____

_____

23 KINGNESS TIP

You're a King. Act like it. Be wise in your decisions.

Penis (Cinquain poem)

Penis

Has seeds of life

Think before you have sex

Protect yourself and your future

Be smart.

23 KINGNESS REFLECTION

You're a King. Be careful of the soul ties you create. Your soul is at stake. Your body is your temple. What standards will you set for your body going forward?

_____

_____

_____

_____

_____

_____

_____

_____

24 KINGNESS TIP

Let the world see you for who you are. Honor your gifts.

Purpose (Cinquain poem)

Purpose

It's your duty

To fulfill your purpose

People need your God-given gifts

Show up.

24 KINGDOM REFLECTION

Stop hiding your gifts and talents from the world. The world needs you King. What is one of your gifts and how can you share it?

_____

_____

_____

_____

_____

_____

_____

25 KINGNESS TIP

You deserve love.

<u>**Finding Love**</u>

It takes courage to open your heart

When it didn't work out in the past

In order to find your queen

You must let that go cause pain doesn't last.

You can't hide behind your emotions

And pretend that everything is fine

Denial will keep you stuck

Allow yourself to heal and give yourself time.

Learn to forgive yourself

Everyone makes mistakes

You can't let the past define you

So don't be afraid to go on a date.

Love wants to find you

And needs you to open up your heart

It's time for you to love again

It's time for a brand new start.

Forgive those that hurt you

So you can move on with your life

You deserve the love that you want

Give yourself permission to get it right.

Dating is a process

Sometimes you win, sometimes you don't

It's best to believe you'll win

So don't think of reasons why you won't.

Your Queen desires your love

Stay the course, you're almost there

The process will all be worth it

You'll have a love that today is rare.

25 KINGNESS REFLECTION

Have you dealt with past hurts? If you don't forgive yourself and the other person, you hold onto old energy which blocks new love. Give yourself permission to love again. What do you need to let go of to love again?

_____
_____
_____
_____
_____
_____
_____
_____

26 KINGNESS TIP

The right partner is out there for you. Speak it into existence.

<u>Love Letter</u>

I know you think about me

As much as I think about you

I know you think about giving up

From all the wrong ones you've been through.

I know you wish I was there with you

And right there by your side

I want you to know you're in my heart

No more tears for you to cry.

I've been praying for you and our future love

Preparing myself everyday

I want to be the best for you

So you feel loved in every way.

I'm not like every other man

My heart will only be yours

I still believe in chivalry

Paying the bills and opening doors.

I believe that you were made for me

What an honor to have you in my life

I won't play any games or take too long

In making you my wife.

I've done the work to heal myself

I will do whatever it takes

I won't be the man to ruin a good thing

I've learned from my past mistakes.

I know I am the King for you

I warn other men in advance

My love for you is already so strong

Other men won't stand a chance.

I promise you it'll be worth the wait

I will find you very soon

Just keep the faith and trust in God

I will love you to the moon.

I am full of hope and believe you're close

We'll share a lifetime of fun things to do

Get ready to be loved like never before

Dear wife, this is my love letter for you.

26 KINGNESS REFLECTION

How are you preparing yourself for your partner? Are your words, thoughts and actions in alignment with what you want?

_____

_____

_____

_____

_____

_____

_____

_____

27 KINGNESS TIP

A well-tailored suit is to women what lingerie is to men.

<u>Clothes</u>

Kings, take a look in your closet

There are clothes that you know you don't wear

There are clothes you've outgrown since in college

Those old shoes show it's time for a new pair.

Your clothes have an effect on your confidence

Your attire is the first thing that we see

If you're trying to make a good impression

It's important to dress appropriately.

None of your clothes should be holey

None of your clothes should have a smell

If you don't take pride in your appearance

The things you want, you are going to repel.

Go out in the world in your Kingness

Let your clothes show the world who you are

No more apathy when it comes to your appearance

You are royalty, represent, you're a star.

27 KINGNESS REFLECTION

Your clothes affect how you feel. You should wear clothes that represent the King you are. How do you feel on a daily basis based on your wardrobe?

_____

_____

_____

_____

_____

_____

_____

_____

28 KINGNESS TIP

Start before you're ready. Build the plane as you fly. You got this, King.

Your Business

King, your vision is your vision

Your dreams are your dreams just for you

Stop letting people who have given up on their own dreams

Negatively affect and dictate what you do.

Start your business, you know that it's inside you

Have faith that God will see you through

God gave you your gifts for a reason

It's up to you what you actually choose to do.

Start your business, your fans are still waiting

Start your business, there's no time to delay

Trust that you will have everything that you need

And whenever you have doubt, just take time to pray.

Have the belief King in your possibilities

You're magnificent as you are in all your being

Please don't live a life without your purpose

Believe in yourself and the fulfillment of your dreams.

28 KINGNESS REFLECTION

You don't have to have it all figured out King. Just take it one step at a time. There's a business inside of you, a product, an idea, something that the world needs. What is stopping you from taking action?

_____

_____

_____

_____

_____

_____

_____

_____

29 KINGNESS TIP

You're a gift from God. Never forget that.

<u>You're Enough</u>

The world may try to tell you

That you'll be enough when you lose ten pounds

No woman would want to love you

When you're short and your stomach is too round.

People may try to convince you

That your current job is a total joke

They talk badly about your ambition

And tell you to give it up cause you'll always be broke.

People may try to tell you

That your clothes are ugly and you have no style

They tell you that your car is too old

You're never enough, not even your smile.

A penis that's small, a pimple to pop

Ears that are wide, will the list ever stop?

People will always judge you

Even if you have a good heart

Do not let their words define you

When it's God that chose you from the start.

There will always be something

That someone can find

You have to love yourself so much

That you keep those haters out of your mind.

You are enough

With all that you are

You are more than enough

You are God's superstar.

29 KINGNESS REFLECTION

You're a blessing to the world King. Please know, believe and remember that. Stop being so hard on yourself and give yourself some credit. What is one thing you're going to do to celebrate yourself?

_____

_____

_____

_____

_____

_____

_____

_____

30 KINGNESS TIP

Every day is a new day. Don't let your past dictate your future. Who you are today and who you are becoming is what matters. You are important. Walk with your head high. Rise up as the King you are.

<u>You're Needed</u>

King, you are important and you are needed

You matter and your presence means so much

Don't worry about the women who claim they don't need you

There are plenty who can't wait for your special touch.

Yes, it is the queen who holds the power

But the queen is incomplete without her king

When you treat her like the royalty that she is

She has no choice but to say yes to the ring.

The man is just as special as the woman

He is a gift and should be loved all the same

There are plenty of good men who want a good woman

Who are done with playing any immature games.

A salute to all the men who are progressing

It takes courage to be yourself and do the right thing

It's easier when you are truly being authentic

Think of the happiness and all the joy that it brings.

Your past does not define you so let it go

Everyone makes mistakes and has lessons to grow.

As long as you understood then you are good

Most of us would things differently if we could.

Kings, you are important and you are needed

We need your faith, your protection and your love

You are blessed when you find us and pursue us

As a man, you are also a gift from above.

30 KINGNESS REFLECTION

Today marks the end of you settling King. You are a gift from God and you matter. We get what we tolerate. Only you hold the key to the manifestations of your hearts desires. You are worthy and deserving of it all. You are a King and will always be a King. You are royalty. Now... What are you going to do differently?

_____

_____

_____

_____

_____

_____

_____

_____

ABOUT THE AUTHOR

Radesha "Desh" Dixon is a poet, model, speaker, pageant titleholder and Forex trader. She is also the author of Queens Don't Settle: A Book of Poems To Empower Women and No More Broken Records: 5 Tips To Change Your Tune and Transform Your Life, both available on Amazon. She is the Creator and Founder of No More Broken Records™, a movement to empower women not to settle; To stop the repeated cycles like a broken record. She believes it's never too late to make positive changes in your life.

She is available for motivational speaking and poetry.

Visit her websites at https://queensdontsettle.com/
https://youdeservefinancialfreedom.com/

Connect with her on social media.

Facebook: https://www.facebook.com/petitewithpurpose

https://www.facebook.com/nomorebrokenrecords/

Twitter: https://twitter.com/NoMorBrknRecrds

https://twitter.com/deshdixon

Instagram: https://www.instagram.com/deshdixon/

https://www.instagram.com/nomorebrokenrecords/

I'd Love Your Feedback!

Reviews are extremely important to authors. If you've enjoyed this book, I'd really appreciate if you'd consider leaving me one. It will help me to share my work with more great men like you!

Thank you so much!

And don't forget –

You're a King. Kings Don't Settle....

Desh

www.ingramcontent.com/pod-product-compliance
Lightning Source LLC
Chambersburg PA
CBHW062049280526
45788CB00003B/1164